HEART'S CRY

HEART'S CRY

MIRIAM NEFF

Tyndale House Publishers, Inc.
WHEATON, ILLINOIS

ISBN 0-8423-0010-4

Printed in the United States of America

01 00 99 98 97 96
8   7   6   5   4   3   2   1

Dedicated to Jeanne Good
my first teacher-sister in the Lord

*Spiritually famished, I drank in your instruction every
Wednesday morning at South Park Church. Your faith-
ful exegesis of every verse, whether Genesis or Malachi,
Matthew or Revelation, primed my spiritual pump
twenty-five years ago. My thirst continues, encouraged
by your example of focused love for God, who has
obviously been Lord of your life.*

CONTENTS

ACKNOWLEDGMENTS

The Tyndale team has earned the perseverance award. Kathy Olson, thank you for sorting through the first ideas, being bold and honest and never giving up. Dan Balow, your vote of confidence encouraged me countless times. Thank you that you see workable ideas in what others might consider dreams. Ken Petersen, I think this book is a milestone in proving Tyndale's ability to flex. And LaVonne Neff, a part of the book's conception—we've finished well together. Thank you for being a mentor who never loses sight of the big picture. You are a treasured friend.

I give you together a team salute. May this book be a blessing.

INTRODUCTION

How would you describe your world? Cluttered with the
trappings of things gone wrong? Smooth on the outside
but wrinkled on the inside from choices in the past? Perhaps you, like me, have come to a time of reckoning in
your life. Life today is a world apart from our little-girl
dreams.

We are a part of the fix-it generation. Bookstores are
crowded with how-tos. We can repair anything. If we cannot repair it, we should have prevented it. We can prevent
anything. Problems in government, schools, families, kids,
careers. It's all-American to work hard, achieve success, be
in charge of life's ladder. This is the American Way.

Stroll with me through a Christian bookstore. The
themes are not much different. In fact, I've written some
of those books. But I am finding that real life is beyond
fixing by figuring it out. If you are a Christian woman
who is divorced, you know what I mean. If you have had
an abortion or had a baby when you were an unmarried
teen, you understand. If your children seem to have made
the wrong choices, if you feel you have failed as a parent,
you *know* that real life is beyond fixing by figuring it out.

Women stumble. Christian women stumble. This book
is *not* about how women go wrong, or why, or which sins

are big or small. You will find no rating scale for bad girls in these pages, no analysis of whose fault it was, no scarlet letters.

This book is for women who know they have stumbled. This book is for women who do not wish to stay down, do not wish to have a life ruled by guilt or by their past. This book is for women who wish to live a successful Christian life.

To be a successful Christian woman is to bring glory to our Creator. Successful Christian women are like search-lights in a darkening world that direct people's eyes to the God of the universe. Successful Christian women are books that others read, and because they have read your book, a God hunger grows within that must be satisfied.

Nothing you have done can prevent you from being a successful Christian woman: no amount of envy or greed that has brought your world down; no hate that has shriveled your soul; no act, no choice. If you are among the 50 percent divorced; were or are an unmarried mom; are one of the 18 percent of Christian women who have chosen abortion; if you are among the one in six Christian adults who has been sexually active outside marriage; if you are substance addicted; you can still be God's successful woman.

Nothing that has been done to you can prevent you from being a successful Christian woman. If you have been abandoned, abused, accused; if your child is born different; if your world has crumbled about you over illness, death, a friend's suicide; you can still be God's successful woman. These events, which invite others to label us as unfortunate or victim or whatever, cannot prevent us from being God's successful woman.

God's woman who has stumbled rises again. She does not stay down. No person—relative, child, lover, employer, coworker—can keep her down. No institution, organization, corporation can keep her from rising.

She rises because she believes.

She rises because she knows the stumbling-success connection.

I write this morning looking out on a frozen world. Another Chicago snowstorm has halted all activity outside my window except for the cardinals at the bird feeder. Two weeks ago I sat in Starbucks with one of my adult children, taking comfort from his presence and the rich aromas of flavored coffees. My chocolate-loving companion, with his chocolate chip scone and hot chocolate, was part of my challenge-filled world at that moment.

I could reach out and touch his hand, his arm.

Today he is in a different place: Department of Corrections, Division Ten. I cannot reach out to touch him, invite him, or bring him home. My real world is beyond my fixing, even if I could figure it out. My life, my family, do not fit the "Christian" formula if that formula is "do it right and God will bless" or "a smooth life is a sign of God's approval."

So as we talk together as women who have stumbled, while I will never tell you that I understand fully your world and your life, I *do* understand being confused. I *do* understand the questions asked in the black night and on the bleak, frigid mornings.

We are not here to survive. "Though a righteous [woman] falls seven times, [she] rises again" (Proverbs 24:16). We are here to rise again.

CHAPTER ONE

Jesus Loves Me

Jesus loves me, this I know.

The simplest truths have the greatest power. Jesus loves me, and I know it. More than a simple truth, it's necessary knowledge in these love-starved days. I once heard a vintage woman say, "Nothing helps me take on a new day like being in a great affair!" She was embarking on another marriage, counting on the adrenaline of this new relationship to carry her through.

As adults we've learned a lot about love: what it delivers and what it destroys. Most of us regularly need a fresh look at what real love is. Otherwise our ordinary living changes our expectations at best or makes us callous and unloving at worst.

Jesus' love is like no other. His love is covenant love: one-way love based on his covenant with us. Rarely does any woman experience a love close to covenant love on this earth. If we consider marriage as one measurement of love, we see from the statistics that it's a contract, not a covenant. Half of all marriages are broken; and of the half that are *not* broken, some could stand some serious patch work.

Here is a word that is not in Jesus' vocabulary: *lovable.* The fact that Jesus loves me is not based on my making myself lovable. He does not love me because of what I've done *to* myself or *for* myself in an attempt to woo him.

Does your mind want to argue with this truth? Mine does. *Miriam, you've got to clean up your act. You've got to perform lovable deeds. You've got to create the right family. You've got to settle into a "nice" lifestyle.*

Jesus loves me, this I know. For the Bible tells me so. Will you take his word for why, when, and how he loves you?

Why

God loved the world, including the women he created, so much that he gave up his Child so that he could have a relationship with us (John 3:16).

God made us as a mirror of himself and said that what he had accomplished was good.

> "Let us make humankind in our image." . . . God saw everything that he had made, and indeed, it was very good. (Genesis 1:26, 31, NRSV)

God loves us because he made us.

> Now this is what the Lord says. He created you, [sister]; he formed you, [sister]. He says, "Don't be afraid, because I have saved you. I have called you by name, and you are mine." (Isaiah 43:1, NCV)

When

All the time.

> "I will never leave you for time or eternity." (Matthew
> 28:20, my personal paraphrase)

God loved us when we'd gone bad like sour milk.

> There is no one righteous, not even one; there is no one
> who understands, no one who seeks God. All have turned
> away, they have together become worthless; there is no
> one who does good, not even one. (Romans 3:10-12)

How

He loves us like we're squeaky clean. And, in his eyes, we are.

> I, even I, am he who blots out your transgressions, for
> my own sake, and remembers your sins no more.
> (Isaiah 43:25)

He loves us with positive protection.

> When you pass through the waters, I will be with you;
> and when you pass through the rivers, they will not
> sweep over you. . . . For I am the Lord, your God, the
> Holy One of Israel, your Savior. . . . Do not be afraid,
> for I am with you; I will bring your children from the
> east and gather you from the west . . . everyone who
> is called by my name, whom I created for my glory,
> whom I formed and made. (Isaiah 43:2-3, 5, 7)

Jesus loves me, this I know. What difference does it make? I
have a bird feeder outside my window filled with sunflower
seeds, millet, wheat, and ground, yellow corn. It's a flurry of

cardinals, bright red and soft pinkish brown, and furry-ball snowbirds painted black, white, and gray. It sways on its tall post with rich provision for each bird who has discovered it. Our recent snow capped it with such a heavy load that the pole leaned slowly to the ground. Now the bird feeder sits on a snowbank, full of seed but birdless. I suppose the cardinals and snowbirds fear taking its provisions because they believe they would be vulnerable on the snowbank. Neighborhood squirrels, our cat, and who knows what other stalkers could reach them there.

God's love is like that birdseed: love we can easily accept when our world is upright and safe. But God's love is still there for us when life has bent us low and we are vulnerable. His love is seed on the ground, in the tallest trees, washing down the Uganzee River. What's safe is being *in* it. Life is taking the love he has to nourish us, no matter how bright the sunshine or how cold and dark the night. What's dependable is *God,* not our location or circumstances.

MY RESPONSE: Care for the Woman in the Mirror

Treat yourself like the treasure you are to God.

Suppose you were given a wonderful creation, full of potential that could accomplish limitless, unusual things. How would you care for this treasure? You would care for it in a way that would enable the wonderful creation to thrive. Fill in the following sentences:

My body needs _____

_____.

My soul needs _____

_____ .

My spirit needs _____

_____ .

God wired you in a special way for a special purpose. Invest in discovering that purpose. Care for your body, soul, and spirit.

Today my body needs _____

_____ .

Today my soul needs _____

_____ .

Today my spirit needs _____

_____ .

If I were to take these actions, my Creator might be more evident in my life and more evident to those around me because _____

_____ .

A few more sentences to complete:

If I could, I would _____

_____ .

In my work, I would most like to _____

_____ .

If I had money to begin a project, I would _____

_____ .

I like to read books that help me _____

_____ .

If I could take a trip tomorrow, I would go _____

_____ .

I have a great sense of comfort when I am _____

_____ .

I am satisfied that I have helped someone when _____

_____ .

I feel I have had a worthwhile day when _____

_____ .

Skills apparent in my work are _____

_____ .

Skills apparent in my relationships are _____

_____ .

As I read about people in the Bible, I relate to _____

_____ .

I connect with this person because she or he is _____

_____ .

I like to work at a job that is _____

_____ .

It is important for me to share _____

_____ .

I like to do something that helps people to _____

_____ .

If I knew how, I would _____

_____ .

If I were a congressional representative, I would _____

_____ .

I would be good at a job where I _____

_____ .

I would like to be famous for _____

_____ .

I have strong beliefs about _____

_____ .

It's important for my family to _____

_____ .

My strongest contribution to my family is _____

_____ .

Consider how God made you unique. Our loving Creator began with a plan. The plan included crafting us in his creative, loving hands to be different from anyone else: body, soul, and spirit. And he said, "She is good."

CHAPTER TWO

Jesus Can Be Trusted

Count on me."

"Trust me."

"I'll be there for you."

What goes through your mind when you hear those words? What do you think if you hear those words from a friend? a salesperson? your mate? Rarely do we hear those words without a background refrain. And that background refrain can either be beautiful or be real sour music.

Our background music has been recorded one day at a time throughout our infancy, childhood, school days, teen years, first job, family, church, first tax bill, first best friend, and first time we were in love.

At some time, as life creates this composition, Jesus enters.

"Trust me."

We hear him with our background music playing.

Little girls who were caught when they leaped to their

daddy's outstretched arms hear beautiful music when Jesus enters their world. For some of us trusting is easy; for others, a lifetime of sour music must be drowned out for us to accept Jesus' love. Maybe you, like me, know how it is to jump at a crucial moment and find that Daddy or Mama is not there. And every day that we have the opportunity to walk with Jesus, that old sour background music tries to play again.

Remember when the little children wanted to come to Jesus? His disciples thought he shouldn't be bothered. Children were so insignificant. But Jesus said, "Let them come."

And they did.

They crawled onto his lap to be cuddled.

He taught a great truth at that moment.

> Unless you change and become like little children, you will never enter the kingdom of heaven. (Matthew 18:3)

People in heaven will be like these children. In other words, those of us who will spend eternity with him are those who trusted, those who climbed onto his lap.

If you feel you can never trust—your life has been too devastated—let me tell you about a piece of land.

Verdun was one of the most heavily contested areas in the First World War. Six hundred thousand men died there in a ten-month struggle that ended in a stalemate. When the armistice was signed, farmers began to fill the trenches and craters. Entire trains were loaded with dud shells, tons of barbed wire, steel pickets, and the skulls and bones of thousands who never had a proper burial.

For twenty years the land resisted all attempts at cultivation. Then someone discovered that Austrian black pines would grow in the lunarlike soil. In 1993, fifty years later, some of these trees were harvested, the stumps were leveled, and hardwoods, like beeches, were planted. In another sixty years those will be cut, and the land will able to be farmed again.

You, like Verdun, are heavily contested territory. The moment you ran to Jesus and climbed onto his lap, the battle was over. However, the soil of your life may need healing. We can trust that Jesus will produce something beautiful, whether Austrian pines, beeches, or wheat. He will decide, in his time.

How do we know this? Because his Word says so:

> No weapon forged against you will prevail, and you will refute every tongue that accuses you. This is the heritage of the servants of the Lord, and this is their vindication from me. (Isaiah 54:17)

> "Though the mountains be shaken and the hills be removed, yet my unfailing love for you will not be shaken nor my covenant of peace be removed," says the Lord, who has compassion on you. (Isaiah 54:10)

> In God, whose word I praise, in the Lord, whose word I praise—in God I trust; I will not be afraid. What can man do to me? (Psalm 56:10-11)

There has never been nor will there ever be a battle in our life that will prevent God from being God.

Jesus taught an important lesson about trust when the children came to him. He said that whoever kept children from him might as well put on a big concrete necklace and jump into a lake (Matthew 18:6). In other words, those who step back when a child leaps, who deceive, who thrive on skepticism and nurture doubt, will not fare well in God's swimming pool.

This is a season when women who believe Jesus need to encourage each other to trust him. Given the current state of affairs in our nation and in our world, nothing else will encourage us to trust. Verdun has produced a forest of sweet-smelling pines. We believe.

MY RESPONSE: Be Courageous

Music in Your Mind: Past

1. List three things your parents told you about yourself in words or actions when you were a child.

_____

_____

_____

2. Describe your first school experience.

_____

_____

_____

3. What important life experiences have created your background music? List these and give a short description.

_____

_____

_____

_____

4. How did these experiences effect your decision to trust Jesus?

_____

_____

_____

_____

Music in Your Mind: Present

1. List three things your parents recently told you about yourself in words or actions.

_____

_____

_____

_____

2. List three things a friend or friends have recently told you about yourself.

_____

_____

_____

_____

3. What has your employer/boss told you about yourself in words or actions?

_____

_____

_____

4. If you have a boyfriend, fiancé, or husband, what has he told you about yourself in words or actions?

_____

_____

_____

5. Describe the background music that results from this information.

_____

_____

_____

_____

Music in Your Mind: Future

1. What does Jesus tell you about yourself?

_____

_____

_____

2. What music does this make in your mind?

_____

_____

_____

3. Which music do you choose to listen to?

_____

_____

_____

Heavily Contested Territory

> [God] devises ways so that a banished person may not
> remain estranged from him. (2 Samuel 14:14)

Just as God is growing trees on Verdun, he has a radical idea
of what can bloom from the soil of your life. He is the tiller
of the soil. Possibilities in your life are limitless. He wishes to
be an intimate partner with you, to work through you.

He will influence your world through the people in your
life, your work, and any other circumstances in which you
find yourself.

What are three opportunities before you where you can
act in a way that would bring glory to your Creator?

_____

_____

_____

What does your background music say about your opportunities? Do you see roadblocks, walls, problems?

_____

_____

What action can you take (or what attitude can you show) regarding these opportunities?_____

_____

    It is easier to keep our distance from God when the going is easy, choices are easy, and there's no contest.

    But eagles fly higher in a storm, trees grow stronger in stiff winds, people develop courage in contests.

    What steps of courage can you take? If the steps seem super-huge, can you take baby steps and at least get started?

    List three things that you can do that are out of your comfort zone that might make a difference for your Creator or bring glory to him in some way.

1. _____

2. _____

3. _____

    Take action. Write on your calendar what you will do. Ask a friend to hold you accountable if you are a procrastinator.

    God does not want you to be estranged from him, weaned from him. Courageous action drains us; we require big doses of spiritual wisdom and energy to keep going. And God delights in our climbing onto his lap, trusting that he'll replenish us for the next step. He delights in see-ing that we trust him enough to leap—to believe there will be a harvest because he knows what he's doing.

When courageous women take action, we send Jesus an all-important message: We're counting on him.

Find a handful of pine needles, and tie them with red string for courage. Place this daily reminder by your kitchen sink, bathroom mirror, or in your work space on the job. You are courageous because Jesus can be trusted.

CHAPTER THREE

Jesus Died for Me

*R*ecently we watched a person we love stand before a judge. One person spoke and handed papers to another. One person recorded evidence, information. We were given the opportunity to speak. We made our plea. It made no difference.

The judge set bond at $500,000. No alternatives, no questions, no chance to go back. The court cleared. Helpless in a fog of no way out. The window of freedom slammed shut.

We talked to a consultant. "Who was the judge?" he asked.

We acquired a lawyer. First question: "Who was the judge?"

We called a friend whom we vaguely remembered had been through this before. "Who was the judge?"

In our fog of confusion we began to get a message.

The judge matters. What matters to him had better matter to us, because he's the judge.

God is a righteous, loving, just, forgiving judge. He can

tolerate anything but sin. And he *is* the Judge. Since he is loving, he gave us a lawyer, called a high priest in Scripture. He gave us Jesus, the Son of God, to stand with us as we approach the Judge.

> For we do not have a high priest who is unable to sympathize with our weaknesses, but we have one who has been tempted in every way, just as we are— yet was without sin. Let us then approach the throne of grace with confidence, so that we may receive mercy and find grace to help us in our time of need. (Hebrews 4:15–16)

God has a world-sized hate for sin. So he set a high price on sin, a price no one could pay. No one can be violent, kill children, cheat the helpless and aged, keep others captive or abuse them and get away with it. No one can lie or take advantage of those who are powerless and escape the consequences. Envy, greed, and jealousy are outside God's tolerance zone. God cannot tolerate people's junk.

Then Jesus steps before the Judge. A half-million dollar bond is like pennies compared to the worth of Jesus. And he stands before his Father on our behalf. Jesus held the only treasure that precious: his own life. He knew the price and he paid it.

One day every one of us will give an account of our lives to our Creator. When we step into the courtroom, a wise question every woman will ask herself is, Who is the judge?

If we have lived as if the Judge were some wise person in history, a human lover, a banker, a philosopher, or a charismatic leader, we will be in for a surprise.

Jesus somehow, some way gets his message to every human: "I'll be in the courtroom. I'll step up to the Judge with you." And every person sends a message to Jesus: "I accept" or "I reject."

Some believe he is the Son of the Judge, which is almost enough. But no price is paid. Some believe he is the Son of the Judge, but they don't think they need his witness. Convinced of their own eloquence, their own charming spin on their life, they approach the Judge alone. Jesus stands silently in the back of the room. What can they offer the Judge?

Believing Jesus died for us is not optional. No woman is free unless the price is paid.

Sisters,

> since we have confidence to enter the Most Holy Place by the blood of Jesus, by a new and living way opened for us through the curtain, that is, his body, and since we have a great priest over the house of God, let us draw near to God. (Hebrews 10:19-22)

Jesus died for us.

What difference does it make to me that Jesus died for me? I sat under an ancient olive tree on the Mount of Olives, near Jerusalem, reading the account of the Crucifixion. Leaning my cheek against the rough, scratchy bark of my shade tree, I thought, *My dear Jesus, this is soft and tender compared to the wood of the cross. You so passionately wanted me to live in freedom that you were willingly arrested and willingly endured beating, humiliation, and pain beyond description. How precious is my freedom to you, my Creator, craftsman of my life. You opened my window of freedom.*

21

I now know the experience of having a brother in the body of believers step forward and pay bond for my loved one. His payment made a statement. His radical act of grace said, "I believe in your future. Having stood before the Judge, you will never be the same. I have great expectations for your life."

My very much alive Jesus steps before the Judge and says, "I offered my life for her bond. I live now so that she may also live."

Jesus lives, and so shall I.

MY RESPONSE: Give Thanks

How do you show gratitude to someone you appreciate?

If you or I had been in a situation where someone literally saved our life, we might be able to comprehend the value of Jesus' choice to die for us. If we had been in a literal prison—perhaps you have—we might be able to comprehend freedom. We can all thank him for what we know he has done for us.

We have a new life today. And eternity beyond imagination. How would you like to thank Jesus for that?

I like to listen to Babbie Mason's song, "All Rise," standing and holding my arms outstretched to show Jesus I appreciate him. One group of women shares answers to prayer and applauds God for each answer. I believe God delights in hearing a whole assembly of women clap for him in gratitude. I think he would also be delighted to hear one woman clap in gratitude.

I confess that thanksgiving is a lost art in my hectic life, especially thanksgiving by recognition. Seldom do I pause to recognize God for who he is and what he's done in our world, our nation, my community, and my individual living space.

Pause for a moment. Look around. What God-prints do you see? I often ask myself, *What God-prints are before my eyes?* Fill in the following sentences with things God has done around you:

1. God has _____

_____ .

2. God has _____

_____ .

3. God has _____

_____ .

I'm sure you could number to twenty and fill each line.

What has God accomplished in your living space? your family? the people in your life?

What has God done in your job—his provision for you to have room and board (as my children say, sleeping inside with bread on the table)?

Taking time to look for God-prints is a valuable exercise.

What do we know about God? Try to think of twenty things.

1. God is _____ .

2. God is _____ .

3. God is _____ .

4. God is _____ .

5. God is _____ .

6. God is _____ .

7. God is _____ .

8. God is _____ .

9. God is _____ .

10. God is _____ .

11. God is _____ .

12. God is _____ .

13. God is _____ .

14. God is _____ .

15. God is _____ .

16. God is _____ .

17. God is _____ .

18. God is _____ .

19. God is _____ .

20. God is _____ .

As I think of God's characteristics, not only am I more thankful, but my faith grows. My mind and heart are reminded that his resources are more than adequate for the challenges in my life. I need to do these exercises because I am forgetful. The daily challenges crowd out the lost art of thanksgiving in my life.

I applaud you, Jesus, for _____

_____ .

I acknowledge you, Jesus, for _____

_____ .

I approve your work in my life because you are _____

_____ .

I recognize that in these circumstances you _____

_____ .

    As we complete these sentences every day, thanksgiving becomes a habit.

Jesus, today I will applaud you by _____

_____ .

Jesus, today I will acknowledge you by _____

_____ .

Jesus, today I will share with _____

_____ that I approve your work in my life.

    The greatest evidence that Jesus has of our thankful attitude is that we love him for what he has done.

> And now these three remain: faith, hope and love. But the greatest of these is love. (1 Corinthians 13:13)

CHAPTER FOUR

The Holy Spirit Comforts Me

And I will ask the Father, and he will give you another Counselor to be with you forever—the Spirit of truth. The world cannot accept him, because it neither sees him nor knows him. But you know him, for he lives with you and will be in you. (John 14:16-17)

When I was ten years old, I slept in a funny-shaped dormer room on the second floor, on the east side of our farmhouse. My sisters had an equally mishapen room on the west side. We were separated by a gaping space that the stairs entered from the lower level. A large, dark hole in one wall was draped with a blanket, and dormers that looked like eyes from the outside let in light, gusts of wind, and a little snow from time to time.

I remember running barefoot up the stairs, through the scary space, into my cozy room to leap into my feather bed. No comforter exists today like the one in my memories. I remember it puffed to over twelve inches high, a delicious depth into which my little body sank gradually, its all-enveloping softness conforming to every angle on my body, including blisters when present. *Comfort.*

Our house burned down when I was eleven. I remember standing in the dark yard, seeing red flames devouring my upstairs room, thinking, *No more rag doll Suzie, no more dress-up clothes.* Neighbors struggled with a hose stretched from the pond, our only source of water. The flames' voracious appetite was unquenchable. I wept over my greatest loss: *My comforter was gone,* no more feather bed. A tiny "comfort vacuum" formed in my soul, small to be sure, but nevertheless real.

Thousands of people today are buying books about comfort, a sure sign that there's a comfort vacuum in our culture. Women's comfort books, couples comfort books, and others are eager to tell you how to know when you need comfort and where to get it.

I've paged through many suggestions on how to comfort yourself, and there are lots of good ideas. Plan your life with more delight, relax, slow down your pace, resolve conflicts, find a support system—good ideas all. Following the directions to comfort may be enough for you.

But our lives do not always allow us time to comfort ourselves. Some conflicts simply will never be resolved on this earth. Some women live daily with an unquenchable fire that relentlessly robs them of comfort, with no way to salvage the feather bed.

So what can a woman do?

Welcome a gift Jesus gave you when you accepted him as your Savior and his Father as your Father. The Comforter, whom Jesus promised to send, is called the Holy Spirit. He is your guaranteed gift, and he's different.

He knows when we need comfort, even if we don't.

He knows us so intimately that he gives us the kind of comfort we need when we're too befuddled to know what we need or how to ask for it. He's a specialist in stroking our soul.

> The Spirit helps us in our weakness. We do not know what we ought to pray for, but the Spirit himself inter- cedes for us with groans that words cannot express. (Romans 8:26)

Those of us who have stumbled in life, who have made large as well as small mistakes, often carry scars, blisters, and bruises from our tumbles. In myself, I am often unaware of an underlying scar until a special circumstance pushes my ballistic button unexpectedly. Then I react with anger more intense than the circumstance merits or with fear that is unreasonable given the facts.

It's OK that I can't figure it out. The Comforter is inside. He knows the scar better than I, and he knows what to whisper in my ear, what to ask for from my Father, how to steer me through the waves of emotion. Like my old feather bed, he gently wraps himself around my blister and is tender with my bruises.

It's a great comfort to know that our success depends only on the Spirit within us. "Not by might nor by power, but by my Spirit," our Lord tells us (Zechariah 4:6). We have little power over fire in our lives and would often feel helpless except for the truth of our Comforter: *I'm in you and will always be here. And because that's the truth, you need no other power.* Our Comforter has come.

MY RESPONSE: Acknowledge and Own My Feelings

The Holy Spirit in me asks Jesus for what I need.

The Holy Spirit asks for what I need, even when I don't know what I need. This incredible Spirit knows it all.

So, sister, do you have a nagging feeling you need something—and you're afraid to own up to that feeling? Why? If you don't tell God, the Spirit will.

So I think I'm too spiritual to need a hug today, too self-sufficient to admit my loneliness, too holy to admit I'm looking too long at someone?

The Holy Spirit knows, and he will ask for exactly what I need in my weakest moments.

I think that frees us to be honest with ourselves, to own our feelings, to admit our weakness.

Finish these sentences:

I wish I didn't feel this way, but _____

_____

_____ .

I'm not proud to admit it, but _____

_____

_____ .

In business we say defining the problem is half the solution. Maybe being honest with God is half the battle. It certainly is a good beginning.

When we need comfort, what is causing the real pain?

My feelings   **Comfort I need**
Envy or jealousy   Comfort for feelings of inadequacy
Embarrassment   Comfort that failure isn't final
Fear   Comfort to face the worst outcome

Fill in some of your own:

My feelings   **Comfort I need**

_____   _____

_____   _____

_____   _____

Comfort for intensely personal pain is often the most elusive because no one has walked our mile.

Facing an illness with no end, a child that cannot be healed, bankruptcy, homelessness—some struggles are so unique that no one we know can relate. No one can say, "I understand." They may say it, but it's not true.

The Holy Spirit is God's answer to this human dilemma.

When no one else understands, maybe no one even knows, the Holy Spirit fills the void. He comforts us

> in all our troubles, so that we can comfort those in any trouble with the comfort we ourselves have received from God. (2 Corinthians 1:4)

Who is in trouble around you?

_____

_____

How can you share the comfort you've been given to pass
on? (Words? Action? Skills? Information? Resources?
Names of people with shared experiences?)

_____

_____

_____

Women are especially gifted at networking.
Who knows how to ?
How can we get this resource to that problem?
We are experts at maximizing the telephone: "Call her.
She might know."
One woman's distress results in salvation for others.
One woman's endurance becomes another woman's
determination.
Just as a child's pain becomes a mother's passion, one
woman's deprivation becomes another woman's drive to
discover provision.

Provisions I can share:

_____

_____

_____

Lord, make me a feather bed in a blistered world.

CHAPTER FIVE

Angels Are Cheering Me On

Connie remembers one time as a child, riding in a station wagon with her grandmother. The car slid over a cliff in the Rockies of Montana, and a pathetic bush projecting from the rock was all that kept them from crashing to their deaths. She was only eight, but she knew with certainty that angels were supporting the station wagon.

One of my sons went on a pilgrimage to New Orleans to "find himself." He left in a fifty-dollar car, the steering wheel taped together with duct tape. Needing money, he sold his car for fifty cents. I could see my man-child in my mind's eye, curled up, sleeping on the sidewalk. To human eyes he was a vulnerable street person. But he was not alone. A wall of angels encircled him, white with glistening wings. And a message went out to the powers in New Orleans at Mardi Gras time: "This is a marked man." And before God, the Giver of the breath he breathed on the

cement of Decatur Street, my son's guardian angel reported
to his Maker every move he made, every danger, every
intervention needed.

What could cheer any mother on more than the knowledge that her children's guardian angels are constantly face-
to-face with God in heaven (see Matthew 18:10)?

In the same way, a woman in today's dangerous world is
never alone. There's more than meets the eye: her invisible
team.

Though unseen, this is no daydream or imaginary crutch
that disappears like white vapor in a blue sky.

Angels are real and powerful and on your side.

Since angels are a different kind of created being,
not like you and me, we may be tempted to doubt
their existence. But we have facts in Scripture to tell us
who they are and what they do. They are an invaluable
part of every Christian woman's team. And given the
times and the tough days in which we live, we want to
be not just knowledgeable, but wisely interdependent
as a team.

What We Know about Angels

Angels are commanded to guard us carefully. They can lift
us so that our feet will not stumble (Luke 4:10–11).

Angels bring provisions to God's people and protect
them (1 Kings 19:3–8).

Angels fight battles for us (Psalm 34:7).

They bring messages (Mary: Luke 1:26–38; other
women: Matthew 28:1–7).

Angels comfort and minister to us (Acts 27:23–24;
Hebrews 1:14).

Scripture reports their activity in the past, from Creation to Jesus' ascension to heaven. Today they are doing the same kinds of things they have done historically. Angels appear to be more active in countries where evil has freer reign than in our country. The salt of our Judeo-Christian heritage has preserved us somewhat for a season. But with the apparent decline of our nation, the activity of angels will likely become more frequent and visible.

We were created lower than the angels, but when we choose to become a Christian, we become a joint heir with Jesus. This intimate position is higher than being an angel. Angels are curious about this—amazed at our relationship with God (see 1 Peter 1:12).

Angels do whatever God asks them to do. We can ask God to direct them to help us or someone else. They can go where we cannot go, at a speed we cannot go.

We can say, "Father, send your angels to protect my daughter on the streets of L.A."

And they are there.

We can say, "Send your angels to surround my son in his prison cell."

And they are there.

They need no map faxed to them to find trouble spots. Their turf is the world.

Thousands of them will sing, "Worthy is the Lamb" one of these days. Why? Because their eyes have seen the supernatural supremacy of God's good power over evil.

Look around you. Nobody there? Look again. Angels are watching you. Angels stand ready to help you. Angels are cheering you on.

MY RESPONSE: Stand Firm

In our "trust what you can see" culture, Christian women can count on power and protection beyond what meets the eye. God has armies of angels waiting to be dispatched at a word from him. Knowing that fact gives me courage. While these armies are directed by God, not us, we can ask God for their assistance. Consider these questions:

1. When can we ask God to send angels to help us?

Anytime. God may use angels or other people, or he may provide a way of escape. Trust him to choose the best method.

2. In what personal circumstances might you ask God to direct angels to help you?

_____

_____

_____

To help another person?

_____

_____

_____

3. Will we see what angels do?

Not necessarily. They may intervene in a place and time unknown to us.

4. What good does it do to ask God to direct angels to help us?

Asking him to send his angels to assist us is evidence of our faith. Our request shows that we believe that he has created beings different from people and has authority over those beings.

Asking him shows that we believe that he wants these creatures to help us. We believe in his ability to accomplish good, using beings that we cannot understand or quantify. That's faith. And God delights to see our faith.

As I prepared to write about angels, I asked several friends if they had had experiences in which they believed angels affected their lives. I heard more than heartwarming stories. I heard of women who were literally saved from death by unseen hands. You might be encouraged by asking friends you know rather well what experiences they have had.

These are not "la-la land" experiences. Rather, these accounts enable us to affirm the scriptural teaching that angels exist and work on our behalf.

Let's acknowledge that truth.

What difference does it make to know that angels are cheering us on? When challenges are before us and we see no solution, we can stand with courage.

We have an unseen army on our side.

CHAPTER SIX

God Loves Me
the Way I Am

How many January magazines are devoted to changing you from head to toe—looks, mood, and attitude?

Dress up for the party. Look professional for the office. Speak softly in this meeting. Be eloquent in this setting. Don't be pushy. You came on too strong. Speak up! Don't you have an opinion? Stifle yourself. That's too much makeup. And that's too little. Stand up straight. Wipe your nose. Color your hair. Wear brighter colors. Dress up. Dress down. You've got to get a different outlook on life. You're too serious. Don't be a heavy. Get real. Take off your rose-colored glasses.

As the messages that we've got to change bombard us, we hardly hear the most significant message being sent to every woman: *I like you just the way you are. You are my friend* (see John 15:15).

Why is this message so significant?

Because as long as we're trying to change ourselves to become likable or different, we're pouring our energy into the wrong project. Jesus wants us to be seasoning in our world, preservative salt in our neighborhood platter, fruit in our malnourished nation. That's what we are to be about. He'll change us so we can change the world.

And there's more. A woman whose focus is on what's wrong with her is unable to see, accept, and use what God has built into her to accomplish either grand or simple things for him. Instead of sensing his affirmation and approval, sensing the freedom to go with what we've got, act with what we have, invest our one or three or five talents, we're scrambling to become different, more likable, like some other woman.

If you and I had been sitting in a college classroom on the campus of William and Mary during the last eight years, we would have seen many women blessed with the charm of youth. Also in the classroom were Jessie Dodge, age eighty-five, and Beulah Walker, age seventy-three. These two women attended classes together for eight years, until Beulah earned her degree and they decided they were too decrepit to make the long, 160-mile round-trip drive two or three days a week.

Did they fit the mold for college students? Hardly. But they accepted their stage in life as one in which they could think, learn, and be challenged. And in the process, they modeled for every young person in the classroom that learning is a lifelong process. Jessie and Beulah showed us in their unique way that age need not be a handicap for the mind.

A woman who sees herself as unlikable or somehow

inferior is like a bush in the wastelands. Scraggly, scrawny, no lush, green beauty, nothing inviting. Consider these words:

> Cursed is the one who trusts in [people], who depends on flesh for [her] strength and whose heart turns away from the Lord. [She] will be like a bush in the wastelands; [she] will not see prosperity when it comes. [She] will dwell in the parched places of the desert. (Jeremiah 17:5-6)

This "scraggly bush" woman is not the one who didn't follow all the instructions in the January magazines. She's the one who turns away from the Lord.

Our Creator is like a potter who takes the genetic pool from every person in our history and shapes, molds, washes down, and reshapes all possibilities for us to be. And he creates a vessel. As the potter's wheel spins and his sensitive hands guide the whirring mass of our being, he detects a tiny flaw. The vessel in process cannot be a vessel for his glory, given that tiny flaw.

So he smashes the pot and begins again. Since all flawed material can be recreated into a beautiful piece of handiwork, it will be gorgeously glorious when he's done, no matter how different the vessel. The Supreme Potter makes it so. He looks with eyes of love at the woman he forms—just the way she is.

Imagine the line at registration for a women's seminar, or a room full of women waiting to apply for Aid to Dependent Children, or models waiting to slink down a runway. Each woman is gorgeously glorious in the eyes of Jesus.

We seem to have an incredible urge to rate people. We don't do this with plants or animals. Pigeons, turtle-doves, snowbirds, and cardinals. Pin oaks, blue spruce, and red maples. Iguanas, chinchillas, platypuses, and giraffes. Salamanders, chameleons, and lizards. Purple thistles, sunflowers, poppies, and asters. Amazing and magnificent partly because diversity intrigues. Diversity is beautiful. So why not accept diversity with people as beautiful, as intriguing?

That's the good news of our Creator. *Yes, woman. Yes, unique vessel. Yes, I like you just the way you are. You have turned your heart to me. You are no bush in the wasteland.* Childish immaturity that keeps us from making a difference has to give way to accepting our sisters just the way they are. No more little-girl games of who's prettier or who's smarter. No more big-girl games of who's more organized, a better communicator, or the fastest fast-tracker. "When I became an adult, I put an end to childish ways" (1 Corinthians 13:11, NRSV).

With that comfort in our soul, we can turn our attention to the reason we are here.

MY RESPONSE: Affirm Diversity

Reread chapter 1, replacing the words *love* and *lovable* with *like* and *likable*. Answer these questions:

1. Why does God like me? _____

_____

_____

2. How does God like me? _____

_____

_____

3. When does God like me? _____

_____

_____

4. How much does God like me? _____

_____

_____

There is only one honest-to-God way to respond. Since Jesus likes us, we can like others. In fact, we can't help but like others. Red and yellow, black and white. Thin hair, fine hair, no hair. Big heart, squished heart, hard heart, or apparently no heart.

When we bask in God's "like" for us, it is impossible for that sense of being nurtured and accepted not to roll over us onto others.

Read about women from other cultural backgrounds. *Never Forget* by Kay Coles James helped me understand my black sisters.

Look for opportunities in your workplace or where you volunteer to get to know women or children who are different from you. The Hispanic girls at the high school where I work have taught me that they value extended family, that illness of elders is important, that a laid-back lifestyle is quality living to them.

Start a breakfast club including women who are different from you. Set an agenda to expand understanding. Begin with a specific time frame—perhaps six breakfasts over a three-month period. Topics might be:

- What were the "favorites" of your childhood (foods, grade school subjects, games, holidays)?
- How did you commemorate important days and events (holidays, birthdays, the last day of school, death of a relative)?
- What did you enjoy reading most (in grade school, in junior high, in high school, as a young adult)?
- What was best about growing up in your family of origin? What was toughest?

Getting acquainted may last through many breakfasts. Then you can begin to grow together—move closer. Topics might be:

- Greatest satisfactions in my life today
- Greatest stresses in my life today
- What I need from other women
- What I'd like to give to other women

Reserve the last meeting to consider:

- What have I learned from our group?
- Have I changed because of our group? If so, how?
- Is there any action I wish to take in the future?

CHAPTER SEVEN

God Will Make Me Better Than I Am

Christian women are in continual motion, a lifelong process of becoming more like our Creator, conformed to his image. How does God accomplish this process in our lives?

As I look at women who bear God's image, I see two factors in their lives: obedience and adversity.

They are Christlike, not because of a self-improvement manual under their arm or a spiritual Day-Timer regulating their experiences. No formulas have produced the spirit that pervades their space.

Rather, they have chosen to say, "Yes, God."

"Yes, God" makes a deep imprint in what they do. They get their answers to questions from the Word of God. They set their moral compass by the same Book. They face life issues, make life choices—as well as small ones—by the Book.

They do so with their mind engaged, with honest dialogue with the Author. Obedience changes them.

How are obedient women better?

Their life, their words, their actions are marked with courage, quiet strength, passion reigned in, emotions that energize rather than raging out of control; and they progress to higher challenges in family, work, or personal development.

They have chosen to face adversity head-on, with a tenacity that requires no spoken "Yes, God." Who they are and what they do with life at its ugliest shouts, "Yes, God." No speech necessary.

> If you have raced with foot-runners and they have wearied you, how will you compete with horses? And if in a safe land you fall down, how will you fare in the thickets of the Jordan? (Jeremiah 12:5, NRSV)

You and I do not struggle through thickets by the Jordan River. But we visit our precious children in prison, we hold our daughters' hands as they bring children into an increasingly dangerous world. Abuse rarely avoids an extended family, and some sisters know its intimate terror firsthand. As Christian women who love God, you and I struggle through our own twenty-first-century thickets of heartache and adversity.

Women looking on see us change. We are better.

Two days ago one of my big bosses ever so gently reminded me, "I've read your books, seen you on television. I've heard you say that parents must stand by their kids in tough times. I know of your faith. Now you are called to *walk the walk.*"

How much more comfortable I am reading the Word in my fireside chair, sipping flavored coffee, snuggling with my purring cat, feet wrapped in comfort. What a far cry from parking on 26th and California before Cook County Corrections, Division Ten, running through the minus- fifteen-degree windchill, showing my license at the gate. I hurry to the next gate, blasted with stinging ice-dust as I cross the open space to the next set of doors. The only thing colder than the Chicago wind is the chill in my heart.

More identification, searched, shoes off, buzzed in, looking into eyes that match mine. I hear in my mind the same words I have said in interviews that reached to hundreds of radio stations: *Stand by your kids. Never give up on them.*

The thickets of Jordan are no playground. We walk the walk. God will make me better than I am. I'm content to race with foot-runners, but God has decided to prepare me for a new kind of race.

Christians in our culture are bombarded with reminders that we are addicted to control.

"I'm in control of my life."

"I can. I will."

"It's my life—my company—my time."

No wonder Christian thought and theology is riddled with the attitude that "we're in control" and "we can make it happen." Contrast that attitude with the following statements:

> "I know the plans I have for you," declares the Lord, "plans to prosper you and not to harm you, plans to give you hope and a future." (Jeremiah 29:11)

> When I am weak, then I am strong. (2 Corinthians 12:10)

Whatever you do, work at it with all your heart, as working for the Lord, not for men, since you know that you will receive an inheritance from the Lord as a reward. It is the Lord Christ you are serving. (Colossians 3:23-24)

This is the day the Lord has made; let us rejoice and be glad in it. (Psalm 118:24)

When adversity comes, what happens to the woman who believes she can make *herself* better? How will she react when

- she loses her job?
- she loses her husband through divorce or death?
- she loses her boyfriend?
- her children make poor or disastrous choices?
- her friends abandon her?
- her financial status drops drastically?

Contrast what happens, in those circumstances, to the woman who believes *God* can make her better.

How does God make us better? He gives us a new heart. Pride is crowded out by humility. Self-confidence is replaced with, "If you're not carrying me, Jesus, I can't go the next *step.* Forget about another *mile!* If you're not in this, Jesus, let me outta here!"

How are we changed?

Finally, all of you, live in harmony with one another; be sympathetic, love as [sisters], be compassionate and humble. Do not repay evil with evil or insult with insult, but with blessing, because to this you were called so that you may inherit a blessing. (1 Peter 3:8-9)

It seems to me that we can learn to live in harmony by the simple lesson of obedience—God says so—and adversity.

"Be compassionate and humble." It takes more than obedience. It's not in us, apart from being carved there through adversity.

With hearts carved open we're better—sisters together.

MY RESPONSE: Rest

Let's get personal. What adversity is staring you in the face?

_____

_____

If you could control every person and circumstance related to the adversity you face, what would you change?

_____

_____

When I do this exercise, I soon discover that I don't have all the answers to fix my problems, even if I could control everything.

What I *can* control is whether I relinquish control to my all-wise Father. Loosening my tight fist and giving God control gives me a new option: to rest in the middle of adversity.

> There remains, then, a Sabbath-rest for the people of God; for anyone who enters God's rest also rests from his own work, just as God did from his. (Hebrews 4:9-10)

According to commentator W. E. Vine, this is a perpetual Sabbath-keeping, to be enjoyed by all believers in their fellowship with the Father and Son, as contrasted to the weekly Sabbath under the Law (*Vine's Expository Dictionary of New Testament Words,* Barbour Books, 1985).

> God will speak to this people, to whom he said, "This is the resting place, let the weary rest"; and, "This is the place of repose"—but they would not listen. (Isaiah 28:11–12)

> Come to me, all you who are weary and burdened, and I will give you rest. Take my yoke upon you and learn from me, for I am gentle and humble in heart, and you will find rest for your souls. For my yoke is easy and my burden is light. (Matthew 11:28–30)

Jesus was talking of rest *in* work rather than rest *from* work. What words describe the woman "resting" while she works? When I rest and relinquish control, I experience

- harmony (in myself and with others)
- peace (underlying assurance that all is well)
- unity of mind and emotions (unfrazzled)
- _____
- _____
- _____

When I am not experiencing harmony and peace, God is sending me a message: *Miriam, are you counting on yourself again or are you counting on me?*

God is committed to making me better than I am. I can rest.

CHAPTER EIGHT

God Made Me One-of-a-Kind

Christian women, in good times and bad, have a secret.

This incredible secret makes all the difference in the world on ordinary days as we go about our business of house care, health care, child care, job care, car care, whatever care. It makes all the difference in the world on extraordinary days when our soul is shouting, *Yea, God!*— days when our dream, the desire of our heart, has become reality.

Our secret perhaps makes the *most* difference on those very bad, very nasty days when our worst nightmares are no longer fuzzy, nighttime fears, but daytime reality. We are awake, and the day is real. Disaster that God did not intend for his beloved woman has struck with the power of a hurricane, the hopelessness of a high wall of water in our face, the finality of a coffin closing.

What is our secret? Simply this: We are incredibly, fearfully, and wonderfully made. We know that every minuscule part of our being was knit together in our mother's womb. The Master Planner of our lives isn't surprised by anything in us. He knew all when he ordained each day, before we experienced our first breath.

He knit our bodies. My daughter, offspring of this mom with wimpy arms, threw the discus on the track team. God knows not only our strengths and weaknesses but also *why* he knit us that way. My friend Mary can live well on four hours of sleep a night. Given the demands of her ministry, The Christian Working Woman, the ability to get along well with little sleep is an excellent strength for God to have given her. My friend Gail's long arms have expanded her world as she navigates in her wheelchair. We are knit together—cable, purl, or any stitch the Master chooses—with good intentions.

He made us one-of-a-kind, and there are no surprises to him about each day. On our good days, we need no convincing that our unique construction is a gift. On the day we discover we passed our bar exam, citizenship test, or driving test, of course we believe our one-of-a-kind construction is adequate and that we can rise to the occasion. For some women, that day is when they discover a baby is on the way, or they finish running a twenty-six-mile marathon, or they move up to a new job.

Does that truth remain on our bad days? Does God retract his statement on days when we crunch our car and we don't know whether we have the patience to face the police, the other driver, the insurance maze, and catching rides to work?

Does that truth remain when our bad days appear for

the moment to be a bad rest-of-our-life? My coworker
Joanne, in her words, has buried two husbands. Losing the
man with whom she thought she'd share a lifetime, at age
thirty-eight with two children, she faced a bleak future. She
never imagined she would go through the same grief again
after nursing her second husband through four years of bed
care. But she did.

I caught up to her after a faculty meeting on Friday after-
noon. With my arm around her shoulders, strong shoulders
that have carried so much, I asked, "What are you doing
this weekend?"

"I'm cooking at the shelter for the homeless. I've
decided to give my life away." One-of-a-kind woman, this
Joanne.

I wonder where a victim mentality fits in to our one-of-
a-kind truth? I couldn't find the word *victim* in my Strong's
concordance. Oh, I know women are identified as victims
in our earthly vocabulary. My guess is that at least a tiny
part of *any* woman's life could be described that way if we
each chose to look for that life space where we were the
casualty, the target, the injured, the one who suffered.

One-of-a-kind women have some tiny strength in some
corner of their soul waiting to be summoned on the day of
darkness. Our Maker has implanted in us something that can
change our perspective so that we're no longer one whose
life is being drained, but rather one who is giving her life
away with unquenchable optimism and determination.

One-of-a-kind women have adrenaline to refocus fear,
whatever their address or life circumstances. Ruth and
Esther did, as did Deborah and Mary, the mother of Jesus.

Some women are created with quiet enthusiasm, others

with outspoken assertiveness. Some with keen eyes and others with good sniffers. Some with strong fingers, others with strong shoulders. Some with critical thinking skills stronger than a bear trap. Others with mellow acceptance of even the most random person on earth. Some, like my walking partner neighbor, have the common sense to see through the foggiest maze of life. Some have an instinct to discern what's really happening in the strangest of life scenarios.

One-of-a-kind women. Each the delight of her Creator, as different as fingerprints, as snowflakes. None more precious than another, the pleasure of God's soul.

MY RESPONSE: Celebrate

What would happen to your world if you rolled out of bed every morning and asked: "What can I celebrate today?"

Today, this one-of-a-kind woman would answer like this:

"Spring! As I ran this morning in the melting snow, there was a twinge of spring in the air, a moist voice whispering, 'I'm coming, I'm coming. I, *Spring,* will arrive.'" More birds were singing after the quiet of freezing weather. I can celebrate spring in the winter air.

I also celebrate motion. (Be it ever so slow.)

What encourages women to celebrate? I am reminded to celebrate when I look around me and remember that nothing exists by chance. Whether in our home, an office, on a street, or in a commuter train, I am awed when I realize that God enabled people to think, to invent, to build, to grow, to manufacture.

Celebrating God is a natural response to knowing that everything around us began at the hand of God.

What do you see around you?

Pick five objects and celebrate God's handiwork in those objects.

1. _____

2. _____

3. _____

4. _____

5. _____

How about celebrating the weather? Will not God smile, even chuckle, to hear us celebrate that which most people complain about? I'll admit that this assignment challenges me. I can celebrate rain; it's cozy. Snow is invigorating and beautiful. Sunshine warms and touches water and ice so they are thrilling. But *fog?* I'll have to work on discovering a reason to celebrate fog! Maybe I can celebrate the fact that it slows us down, and that's not bad.

Celebrate circumstances and the positive possibilities that might happen. While positive thinking does not guarantee perfect days, those positive thoughts are more likely to highlight the good in any situation.

Describe a relationship that is important to you.

_____

_____

_____

What positive possibilities might be in the future of this relationship?

_____

_____

_____

Celebrate that person.

Celebrate the relationship.

How can we celebrate circumstances that seem negative at the moment?

Celebrate God, who knows tomorrow can be better. Sometimes newscasters, economic forecasters, and even spiritual leaders predict gloom and doom. While I can agree that our economy may be on a downward trajectory and the spiritual vitality of our nation may be headed down even faster, God is still God.

For us as Christian women, there is more to the quality of our lives than our economic status. Our spiritual fervor need not diminish to match that of our nation or even our local body of believers. Women in Scripture repeatedly model how to live above negative circumstances.

Celebrate God who will give us opportunities that match our one-of-a-kind strengths. What opportunities might match your strengths?

_____

_____

_____

Celebrate God who will give us grace to cover our one-of-a-kind weaknesses. What illustrations of grace do you see in your life to cover your weaknesses?

_____

_____

_____

God's grace in my life consists of friends who balance my impulsiveness. They gently advise me and draw me to think of the big picture. God's grace includes a dependable husband who covers my weakness to fear abandonment.

As you and I list illustrations of grace in our lives, let's celebrate God's wisdom.

Celebrate God who defines *victim* as one who can be healed, one who will rise again because her Creator can make her stand when her knees are feeble and her ankles twisted. His loving arms are tucked under hers, and she feels his tenderness.

Celebrate the fact that your sisters are not just like you. Celebrate that God made each of us one-of-a-kind.

CHAPTER NINE

Jesus Will Love Others through Me

We can find ever so many idea books to expand our love actions and vocabulary. *101 Ways to Love Your Child. 101 Ways to Love Your Husband. 365 Ways to Tell Your Teen You Care.* Humans never give up in their creative quest for ways to communicate love. Hearts and initials painted high on train trestles. A girl holding a large hand-painted sign at a corner as her boyfriend's bus speeds by. A young man plotting with a local policeman to stop his girlfriend and issue her an engagement ring.

How to show love, though sometimes a challenge, is not the greatest obstacle in spreading the greatest positive power on earth.

Who—to whom—seems to be where we humans stumble.

Nothing expands the scope of whom you see as lovable as much as tragedy in your life. In my own job as a high school guidance counselor, it was always easy to help clean-cut, cooperative kids who fit in and flowed with the system. And then my own children blossomed. And with the training ground of my heart deeply tilled, I now have love for many different kinds of people.

Hyperactive kids, who sit in my office banging their feet repeatedly against my desk, look lovable to me. Thin boys with nicotine stains on their fingers. Young men with shaved heads and anger in their eyes. Girls with a chip on their shoulder of distrust for the system I represent. These kids all look lovable to me.

Women who weather rough places love different people after their walk through the rain. And that's good. Does it sometimes seem like more good stuff comes to the folks who have enough already? Those of us who have weathered the stuff of life can change that perception. We can show that good things come from tough circumstances. Rather than retreating into our world of hurt, fearing possible rejection or misunderstanding or judgment for our unique circumstances, we can take the love with which our Creator sustains us and go public.

Carmella LaSpada went public with love that grew from her visit to Vietnam in November 1967. A medic of a group known as the Black Scarf battalion described to her his experience as thirty-five of his buddies died around him. He had run from one dying man to another doing all he could do to soothe their pain. This medic took off his black scarf and placed it around Carmella's neck. He asked her to do what she could to remember them.

At first she felt immobilized by the grief of hearing this tragic story. Then she decided to do what she could. She decided to love the children of fathers who would not be coming home. One six-year-old had run home from school one day crying, "Mommy, Mommy, Daddy isn't a murderer, is he?" The gifts, letters, and photos from Carmella changed him. This confused young boy and other children began to develop a sense of self-esteem when they needed it most because Carmella loved them.

She established special children's ceremonies on Memorial Day and a Father's Day ceremony after the Vietnam Memorial Wall was built. Jesus was loving others, touching them in a special way, through the woman who had talked to the medic. *How* she showed love to the children changed as the children changed. But *whom* to love was determined by the experience her Maker took her through.

For God so loved the *world* . . .

Is everybody getting some of his great passion? Are some hiding behind a curtain of failure when the hugs get passed out? Are some buried beneath layers of poverty's blankets—the wrong look, the wrong smell, the wrong attitude?

Jesus will love *others* through me.

Our world quivers, and a new horizon appears before us. New people, not necessarily of our choosing, appear in our life space. Some we are easily, automatically drawn to. Others? Well, Jesus will love others . . . *through me.*

I am just a vessel. It's his love they need, not my puny passion. My part is to be willing to be the vessel. The rest is up to him. We could never know how to love another. But God, who knows their need, sure does. And he will prompt us to action as he did Carmella LaSpada, and my coworker Joanne, and the thousands of other women throughout the centuries who have softened the toughness of this world with their love in action.

MY RESPONSE: Encourage Others

A present-day model of a woman who encourages others is Barbara Johnson, author, speaker, and especially encourager. Out of her own tragedy—the deaths of two of her sons and the homosexuality of another—she wrote her first book, *Where Does a Mother Go to Resign?* She writes of the real stuff of her life with touches of humor.

In addition to writing and speaking, she answers bags of letters every month and publishes a newsletter. I spoke with one of her publicists about Barbara's special gift of encouraging. "When Barbara asks you how you're doing, no matter what's happening around you and how many people are there, you know she's listening just to you. She makes you feel that you are most important. She *hears* you."

Barbara has rediscovered one of today's forgotten methods of encouragement: listening.

I sometimes mistakenly believe that if I listen to someone's problem or hurt, I need to fix what I've heard. Listening is scary when you believe you need to carry your tool kit and solve everyone's problems.

You and I can let ourselves off the hook. God is the Great Deliverer (Psalm 34:17). Our task may be to listen or perhaps to pray. Yes, we may need to take action, but not necessarily.

If you want to be an encourager, consider the following:

- Is there someone in my circle of friends and acquaintances to whom I could listen?
- When I need a listener, what responses encourage me most?

- Who is least likely to have a listener? Can I be a listener to someone who is seldom heard ("The Lord hears the needy and does not despise his captive people." Psalm 69:33)?

The Golden Rule offers a good lesson in encouragement:

In everything, do to others what you would have them do to you, for this sums up the Law and the Prophets. (Matthew 7:12)

What encourages you to reach your personal goals? List your goals in the following areas:

1. Relationships

_____

_____

_____

2. Family

_____

_____

_____

3. Professional development

_____

_____

_____

4. Personal learning

_____

_____

_____

5. Spiritual growth

_____

_____

_____

What would encourage you in each of these five areas?

1. Relationships

_____

_____

_____

2. Family

_____

_____

_____

3. Professional development

_____

_____

_____

4. Personal learning

_____

_____

_____

5. Spiritual growth

_____

_____

_____

For each area below, write in the name of a friend, relative, or coworker whom you can encourage as you would
like to be encouraged.

1. I can encourage _____ in this relational

area by _____

_____ .

2. I can encourage _____ in her family

challenge by _____

_____ .

3. I can encourage _____ in her professional

development by _____

_____ .

4. I can encourage _____ in her personal growth by _____

_____ .

5. I can encourage _____ in her desire for spiritual development by _____

_____ .

Have you ever been encouraged simply by observing another person? I have. A great encourager in my life was Bible teacher Jeanne Good. I was encouraged by her example as much as by any specific acts of encouragement. She studied the Word. She faithfully taught in two locations week after week, month after month, year after year. Who she was as a Christian woman encouraged me.

In these busy days when preparing homemade bread may be a nearly impossible way for us to encourage a sister, just *being* a daughter of God sends a message.

One of my busiest friends, Jan, encourages me by loaning me books for my spiritual growth. During our rare moments together, she'll say, "What did you think of that book? Here's what I learned."

Recommend refreshing movies or good biographies. Fax a cartoon. Leave an "I'm thinking of you" message on her voice mail. Life may be busy and moments full, but make use of the technology at hand to help you encourage others.

CHAPTER TEN

Jesus Affirms My Potential

There is no greater wind beneath your wings than the knowledge that someone believes in you. Kids do better in school when teachers think they are smart. Husbands wash dishes cleaner, toddling babies try to stay on their feet longer. How sweet those words, "You can do it."

Watch a relay. Every runner is energized by the team. Some races are won seemingly by the sheer energy and electricity of the support in the stands.

One of the greatest losses for Christian women when we blunder is the loss of that synergy around us—the support, the encouragement to go on. Not only do we struggle to believe in ourselves, we may struggle alone because others are disillusioned by our failure.

We know the sense of defeat when we fall. How can we rise again, especially when others become skeptical or distant?

Jesus affirms our potential.

He never gives up on us and persistently tells us so.

- "I expect great things from you, sister."
- "You can do anything through me" (see Philippians 4:13).
- "My words will make you wiser than your enemies" (see Psalm 119:98).
- "If you stay as close to me as you can, I won't let you make a mess of things" (see Psalm 119:31).
- "Watch my performance today, through you, daughter."
- "Watch me make these knots into an heirloom tapestry" (see Romans 8:28).
- "I know and understand what is best for you at all times" (see Jeremiah 29:11).
- "Look what's out there, sister. It's you; you can do it. *You* are going to bring glory to my name. Yes, *you.*"
- "Look where I'm pointing, sister. See the future I have called you to share" (see Ephesians 1:9)?

And we stand, oh, so close to him and focus in the direction he is pointing: beyond the mess that just tripped us up; over the wall of discouragement and fatigue; beyond our starter kit of skills.

Granted, it is surely grand to have a support system of thousands—those who believe in you and expect you to do well. But a support system on earth is not one of God's guarantees. Jesus is it. And we must never forget it.

When I read stories of missionary women who have been out somewhere alone, facing every danger imaginable and still bringing glory to God, I wonder, *What if she had stayed here? What good might she have done in our country for God's glory?*

Possibly not as much. Just maybe her strength was from getting close to Jesus alone and focusing on where his loving arm pointed. Gazing beyond his fingertip to the goal that he trusted her to reach. Jesus affirming her potential.

Catherine Booth, the cofounder of the Salvation Army, heard this prompting from the Holy Spirit: "If you were to go and testify, you know I would bless it to your own soul as well as the souls of the people." Yet, she felt she could not do it. She believed the devil whispered to her that she was unprepared and would look foolish. She chose, however, to act on the affirmation of the Holy Spirit. Thirty years later, the following was said of her: "No man of her era exceeded her in popularity or spiritual results, including her husband" (Ruth Tucker and Walter Liefeld, *Daughters of the Church* [Grand Rapids, Mich.: Zondervan, 1987], p. 264).

There is a tiny little word in Scripture that packs a great punch: *if.*

- If faith isn't accompanied by actions, it's dead (see James 2:17).
- If you ask in my name, you will receive (see John 14:13-14).
- If a woman eats the bread I supply, she will live forever (see John 6:51).
- If Jesus affirms our potential, why would any woman stay down when she stumbles?
- If Jesus affirms our potential, why do we say, "I can't"?

- If Jesus affirms our potential, what kind of stuff are we made of?

We have within us all the makings of that woman Jesus is counting on, that woman who will bring glory to God in the future, in circumstances we would shrink from today. That woman who will bring glory to God is the woman in the mirror.

MY RESPONSE: Take Risks

Take time to read about Christian women in history. *Daughters of the Church* by Ruth Tucker and Walter Liefeld is an excellent beginning.

What risks did Christian women take in the past?

_____

_____

How are risks different today?

_____

_____

How are they the same?

_____

_____

Select women from the Bible. I read about Hagar, Miriam, or Esther and ask the same questions.

What risk did Hagar take when she returned home after running away with Ishmael (Genesis 16)?

_____

_____

What risk did Esther take when she appeared before King Xerxes (Esther 4–5)?

_____

_____

What risks did Mary the mother of Jesus take (Matthew 1–2)?

_____

_____

What do you fear most when you face choices ahead?

_____

_____

_____

My list of fears includes looking foolish and losing financial security. When I hold these fears to the truths of Scripture, I have nothing to fear at all. I would rather be the world's biggest fool than a slouch or a wimp in God's army of courageous women. I would rather enjoy God's blessing in personal poverty than have wealth in a life space remote from him.

As long as my risks are ambiguous fears, I hesitate to face them. When I write them down, they become specific choices. There is Scripture that teaches me how to face that fear and promises solutions based on who God *is,* rather than on my observable circumstances.

As you assess choices, you may have a smorgasbord from which to choose. Every choice is accompanied by risks. *A Time for Risking,* by Miriam Adeney, offers insights into priorities for women today. Her insights may help you choose. She challenges us to set priorities more "other directed," like helping teens, caring for the poor, and being advocates for those who cannot help themselves.

I need those reminders in my world. An invisible magnet seems to draw my attention inward to my small circle, my family, and my own personal issues.

Risk taking is not an end in itself for Christian women today. Magazines at the checkout counter encourage us to take risks for self-fulfillment or for the thrill of testing limits. Our efforts will dwindle quickly if that is our motivation. The Christian woman takes risks based on what her Creator has called her to do.

Jesus affirms our potential for a reason. He has a job for us to do and that job is simple: We are to tell the world about him. As sisters working together to accomplish this great commission, he gives us direction.

> Therefore encourage one another and build each other up, just as in fact you are doing. (1 Thessalonians 5:11)

Jesus has given us the gift of himself and challenges us to risk anything to give this gift away.

CHAPTER ELEVEN

God Has Forgiven Me

How can I get close to God? His Father-love is so compelling that I want to be as close as I can be. No intimate relationship has higher priority than God and me. In our I-can-do-it-myself world, I begin to calculate how to make it happen. How can I get into his inner circle? What are my options to earn my way in? Roadblock after roadblock barricades me from God.

Messages about what works in this world resonate in my ears:

- "Perform, perform, perform. Accolades and applause to the best and the brightest."
- "If you really shine on this project, we'll talk about promotion."
- "After you clean your room, we'll discuss your allowance."
- "Let's look at your sales record before we talk about the new team."

How delightfully shocking to find that God is not impressed by performance. He is neither driven to promote us, nor discouraged from blessing us, by our resume. Neither a string of earned credentials and accomplishments nor blunders, bloopers, and downright life-crushing messes dictate God's acceptance or rejection of us.

> Therefore, [sisters], since we have confidence to enter the Most Holy Place by the blood of Jesus, by a new and living way opened for us through the curtain, that is, his body, and since we have a great priest over the house of God, let us draw near to God with a sincere heart in full assurance of faith, having our hearts sprinkled to cleanse us from a guilty conscience and having our bodies washed with pure water. (Hebrews 10:19-22)

"What—*me* talk to God based on what Jesus has done? Intimacy that I don't have to earn? I've made more than a few messes in my life. In fact, right now, I'm not squeaky clean."

"You mean, God himself wants to see me?"

I imagine a special room, cozy with a soft, tapestry drape door. Before Jesus gave himself away for you and me, the curtain was a barrier keeping me out. Jesus lifts the barrier and beckons to me.

"Thank you, Jesus." Thanks for holding up the curtain.

That smile on God's face. He's really glad to see me, isn't he?

My steps quicken. I run.

I crawl into his lap. His welcoming arms.

Thank you, Jesus, for more than an invitation—for opening the door.

As I bask in the total acceptance of my Father, a tiny fear creeps in. Will my past enter this special room and give witness to messes in my life? Will my Father push me from the lap of his favor? Will Jesus ask me to leave?

> As far as the east is from the west, so far has he removed our transgressions from us. (Psalm 103:12)

> Praise the Lord, O my soul, who forgives all your sins and heals all your diseases. (Psalm 103:3)

Just as the east will never intersect with the west, my sins will never intersect with God. Jesus stands between my failure and my perfect Father. The two will never collide.

When a young girl who has led a good, pure life becomes a Christian, Jesus' sacrifice covers any wrong she has imagined or done. A mature woman, scarred by a lifetime of terrible choices, aged with the filth of being trapped in any wicked system—whether behind the facade of a cult, bad business, or a sick family—is washed just as pure and white, just as wrinkle free, just as squeaky clean as the young girl.

Their bodies may look different, but their sprinkled hearts are equally clean.

I recently met a woman who delights in visiting women in jail. Her eyes sparkled with an enthusiasm for her work, evidencing rare zeal. Single now, though she has had four husbands, her time is hers to give away. Her only child was killed at age twenty-two. This woman's life story is a vivid living example of Jesus' observation that she who is forgiven much, loves much (see Luke 7:47).

No wonder the women she visits look forward to her coming. She exudes hope. She is hope in the flesh. She has a message beyond the reason for the scars from abusive relationships in her past. She carries the message of God the Great Forgiver, Jesus the Redeemer. They hear her story and say, "Yes, God wants to see me. Jesus lifts the curtain and invites *me.*"

MY RESPONSE: Forgive Others

God did not wait for me to clean up my act before forgiving me. I confess that I am more willing to forgive someone who has apologized, made restitution, and vowed to never need my forgiveness again. Whether it be my child who promised never to run past the coffee table again with his Superman cape flapping over my treasured figurines, or an acquaintance who promised he would wisely utilize our money in his new entrepreneurial endeavor.

With figurines shattered on the floor and my bank statement reading zero, I have the opportunity to learn forgiveness.

> But God demonstrates his own love [argues his love] for us in this: While we were still sinners, Christ died for us. (Romans 5:8)

Whom do I need to forgive today? If you and I make a list, they might be similar.

my child because _____

_____

my coworker because _____

_____

my relatives who _____

_____

my mate, who _____

_____

my mother/father for _____

_____

Your list might include a stepparent, a neighbor, a former friend, or even a stranger whose choices have affected you somehow. Any month of normal living produces dozens of opportunities to forgive.

Now I imagine Jesus talking to each person I need to forgive.

What would he say to my child? my coworker? my former friend?

Rare, refreshing, like no other. This Jesus has some kind of forgiving love. This same Jesus then turns from those I need to forgive and gazes intently at me.

> Why do you notice the little piece of dust in your friend's eye, but you don't notice the big piece of wood in your own eye? How can you say to your friend, "Friend, let me take that little piece of dust out of your eye" when you cannot see that big piece of wood in your own eye! You hypocrite! First, take the wood out of your own eye. Then you will see

clearly to take the dust out of your friend's eye.
(Luke 6:41–42, NCV)

If I laid down the planks from my own eyes, I could start a woodpile. Imagine the defensive walls that would come down if sisters saw each other laying the plank of jealousy on the woodpile, the plank of promiscuity, the plank of indifference to the plight of children?

Imagine our improved vision after building the woodpile. We would see our sisters and brothers with sawdust in their eyes stumbling on the same journey we are on. I confess that even among Christian sisters we rate some sins as more acceptable, more "politically correct," more forgivable than others. I tolerate jealousy in myself but not indifference in someone else.

If we could see as God sees, we would see hypocrisy as another plank to lay down. We would see our sisters who have chosen to have abortions and those who are homosexuals as women God loves, women who in God's eyes are just as forgivable as we are.

What sins do I rate as *big?*

_____

_____

_____

_____

_____

The same Jesus who loves me so much that he lifted the curtain separating me from his Father wisely advises me:

Do not judge, and you will not be judged. Do not condemn, and you will not be condemned. Forgive, and you will be forgiven. Give, and it will be given to you. A good measure, pressed down, shaken together and running over, will be poured into your lap. For with the measure you use, it will be measured to you. (Luke 6:37–38)

This same Jesus who lifted the curtain for me is the only one qualified to do so for each precious person.

CHAPTER TWELVE

God Has Cleansed Me

The Dead Sea in Israel is 26 percent solid ingredients, including salt, sulfur, petroleum, and bituminous matter, while most bodies of water are 4 to 6 percent solids. The Dead Sea has no outlets; water leaves only by evaporation, keeping it mineral laden.

Being the tourist who must try everything, I wore old shorts and a T-shirt for the adventure of floating on the Dead Sea. And it was quite an experience. Even being especially buoyant, floating high in the water, I got occasional splashes which stung my eyes and tasted sickening. A little swim was enough, and I was grateful for a shower to rinse off the drying accumulation of salt and sulfur. In my customary hurry, I skipped the shampoo in order to get on to the next adventure.

As the dry air of the Middle East performed its normal function, my beehive (the fashion statement at that time) stiffened into a sagging pyramid glued to the back of my head that no finger could dent, no comb could straighten.

I learned a lesson that day about cleansing. It was not enough to get out of the Dead Sea. I had to rinse thoroughly, to have pure water wash over my whole being *after* getting out of the mineral-laden water.

Forgiveness, while a miracle for which I will be grateful forever, is not enough. Our Creator knew we needed to be clean in order to live the life he has planned for us. And we are clean because he says so (see John 15:3). In fact, even our conscience is clean (see Hebrews 10:22).

Do you find that your conscience is a rebel and does not want to keep in line with what Jesus has promised you? Mine is. My conscience specializes in trying to load guilt on me that immobilizes me from energetic, free-to-serve, Christian living.

Like the chemicals in my hair after my swim in the Dead Sea, guilt is a weight that I need not carry.

One of the weights of guilt is the lie that the messes of our past will prevent God from using our present and future life to his glory. Thank God he is not a puny god; nothing we do controls or restricts him. Not only is he completely able to create a beautiful present and future, he is even able to change the results of the past.

Our days or months or years that were gobbled up by messes we made, circumstances beyond our control, or tragedy may look like times of drought to us and to others, but God does not see life that way.

> I will repay you for the years the locusts have eaten—
> the great locust and the young locust, the other

locusts and the locust swarm—my great army that I
sent among you. You will have plenty to eat, until
you are full, and you will praise the name of the
Lord your God, who has worked wonders for you;
never again will my people be shamed. Then you
will know that I am in Israel, that I am the Lord
your God, and that there is no other; never again will
my people be shamed. (Joel 2:25-27)

God looks at days in our lives eaten by locusts as opportunities for replacement. And he begins by cleansing. He
loves a good shower. I imagine him smiling down on Chicago when he sees his rain wash the streets, cleanse the
smell of O'Hare from the skies, rinse the emission junk
from the leaves in Lincoln Park. Would he delight any less
in our personal cleansing?

On my sightseeing day with my beehive of iron, I learned
another lesson about cleansing. Cleansing *quickly* is the best
policy. By the end of that hot day, my hair was not only
ashen gray, it had become dry and brittle. While a shampoo
never felt so good, more than a few handfuls of conditioner
were needed before my hair was manageable again.

Jesus promises immediate cleansing at the same time as
forgiveness. It's a fact we can count on.

In a present, painful circumstance in my life, I am powerless to change an ongoing, unjust circumstance. As bad
news continues to come like one wave pounding in after
another, the refrain of a song has rung in my mind: "Lord
of all, Lord of seen and unseen things." Joel says that I will
praise the name of my Lord. I need not praise these dread-
ful circumstances. Thank God for that. In faith, I can praise

his name. Praising his name is not beyond this daughter of God, even while the locusts are still munching about me.

Praising God has an immediate cleansing effect. Praise cleanses bitterness from our heart and depression from our mind. Praise scours out hopelessness. The "Lord of all" is the Lord of showers for women who have just emerged from swimming in the Dead Sea.

MY RESPONSE: Disconnect from the Dirt in My Life

> Throw off everything that hinders and the sin that so easily entangles, and let us run with perseverance the race marked out for us. (Hebrews 12:1)

One of the great comforts in Scripture is that ordinary advice spills over every page, words that acknowledge that what I'm experiencing is normal and therefore treatable. During Jesus' time, women struggled with many of the same issues common to us today.

The saintly scholar who wrote Hebrews knew that even when I'm motivated to run, snarly vines grow over my path. I emerge like Lazarus from the grave, with new life but bound by graveclothes. They must be loosed before I can run.

Our sins may be hidden from people, but they are no surprise to God (1 Corinthians 10:13). I look in Scripture and see that the same vines that grow around my feet were growing thousands of years ago.

Sibling Rivalry
Read Luke 10 about Mary and Martha.

What were Mary and Martha's differences?

_____

_____

How did Martha overcome sibling rivalry?

_____

_____

Is there a lesson here for me about relationships with my sisters? my brothers?

_____

_____

Disappointment with the Heritage I Received from My Family
Read Luke 15 about the elder brother and the Prodigal Son. While this parable is about two brothers, it could easily describe two sisters today.

What choices did the elder brother have regarding his relationship to the returned younger brother?

_____

_____

What choices did he have regarding his relationship with his father?

_____

_____

What were the attitude options for the elder brother?

_____

_____

One way to disconnect from bitterness related to family is to focus on our new family and our new heritage with our heavenly Father.

Lifestyle and Behavior Outside God's Guidelines
Read John 4 about the woman at the well.

What could the woman at the well change about her past?

_____

What can you and I change about our past?

_____

_____

Habits That Have Become Comfortable though Not Helpful
Read Mark 10:17-27 about the rich young ruler. Contrast the rich young ruler and the woman at the well.

Describe the rich young ruler's comfort zone.

_____

_____

What were his choices?

_____

_____

The woman at the well eagerly became a representative for Jesus. We do not know whether the rich young man became a believer or not. He does illustrate the difficulty of leaving our comfort zone.

Questions to ask about my habits:

- Does this bring me closer to my Creator or drive us apart?
- Does this action move me toward my goal of bringing recognition to my Creator, or does it bring recognition to myself? Does it bring recognition to some other person, and is that appropriate?
- If the action appears to be OK based on these criteria, are there still better uses for the time, energy, and attention that this habit consumes?

I am encouraged to know that falling when running this race does not signal my failure. Dirt exists in real living, and I cannot always skirt it, leap over it, or run through it unscathed. But I will not stay down. God's promise to me is that I will rise again.

> For though a righteous [woman] falls seven times, [she] rises again, but the wicked are brought down by calamity. (Proverbs 24:16)

I am forgiven and cleansed at the same time.

If I accept the fact of my forgiveness but ignore the reality that I am cleansed, I am more likely to live with tarnished choices in my own life. Accepting the fact that I am clean as well as forgiven motivates me to act like a cleansed woman.

CHAPTER THIRTEEN

God Will Soften My Heart of Stone

Time can toughen or tenderize. A pliable young tree can bend in a storm and straighten again. A baby can wrap his foot behind his neck and use his ankle as a pillow. (Sounds painful, doesn't it?) Two young people, newlyweds, as different as can be, can marry and adapt to each other's idiosyncrasies.

On the other hand, a tree can succumb to time and become petrified, bearing the imprints of plant life or animals from years before. Our bodies can become brittle, unable to bounce with the bumps of life. Two married people through shared years can grow intolerant and unable to go with the flow of life together.

Tenderness is not a natural by-product of passing time. In fact, it is more likely that under normal circumstances we will become tough rather than tender. I don't see our world becoming sweeter; the systems of education, law, or government becoming smoother; or the stuff of life taking on a more pleasant savor.

As I look at the progress women have made in our country, in our culture, I see that we have greater freedom and opportunity than most women who have existed on this planet. Yet even with this tremendous progress, I hear women speak with anger about our status today.

Our lives are not all they should be, without question.

And our lives are certainly not all they will be.

Still, Scripture leaves no room to doubt that we are to be tenderhearted, compassionate.

> Be kind and compassionate to one another, forgiving each other, just as in Christ God forgave you. (Ephesians 4:32)

I shall never forget Corrie ten Boom's story of the guard who was so cruel to her and her sister in the concentration camp during World War II. After her sister's death, Corrie was finally freed to begin again. Her new life of freedom could have been shackled with bitterness and anger, and justifiably so.

When Corrie later unexpectedly encountered this cruel guard, she was miraculously able to forgive him. Apart from the significant impact her forgiveness had on the guard, it made a world of difference to Corrie herself. Her life after the camp was marked by sharing God's goodness, including the miracle of forgiveness. Those who met her caught her passion for God—not because time passed and she forgot the evils of her life, but because she *chose to forgive*. God wished her to do so. And she did.

Tenderness is all about what happens in time.

The process of first sinning, then recognizing our stumbling, and finally acknowledging God's incredible ability to forgive us is the only thing that can create a tender heart. Recognition of our own fallibility enables us to forgive others for being less than perfect.

If our life had not been tattered, we would not know the delight of a mended soul.

If our relationships had not been shipwrecked, we would not know the pure pleasure of a restored friendship.

If our wounds had not been healed with forgiveness, we would not know the miracle of recovery.

Kay Coles James suffered from racial discrimination as a grade-school student during a busing experiment to integrate schools. Today she is a vivacious Christian leader and a positive political activist.

Linda Rios Brook was once fired from a prestigious position because she believed Jesus was who he said he was. She found herself the butt of media jokes and unemployed because of her faith. Today she is a television station owner and manager, leading a family-friendly operation. She still makes time to teach Bible classes and is an electrifying speaker.

These women chose to forgive, and it has made all the difference in their lives today.

Time allows us to contemplate what life would be like without God, who has the power to bring positives from negatives.

Time gives the gift of appreciating that change is as sure as the sun's rising—and that God, who made the sun to rise, just might have a hand in change.

Time offers us the opportunity to look around us and examine our world for evidence of the Creator of all.

Remember that over time, Verdun became productive farmland again rather than permanent wasteland.

A strong heart is not the one made of steel but rather a God-softened, tender one of trust.

MY RESPONSE: Own the Lesson and Share
What I've Learned

While there may rightly be a debate among believers about how much self-revelation is appropriate, we can say with confidence that many struggles equip Christians to share with others what God has done and how he did it.

> The Sovereign Lord has given me an instructed
> tongue, to know the word that sustains the weary.
> (Isaiah 50:4)

God gives us an "instructed" tongue, not a torpedo. He gives us a mission to "sustain" the weary, which means we do not always mend, produce a miracle, or permanently fix anyone else's life.

Rather we support them, uphold them, defend them from the relentless discouragement in their life struggle. Where do we begin? The body of believers does a good job of sharing food with those in need. While food does not repair the broken car of the single mom with hungry kids or the broken heart of a widow, it is a good beginning and carries the encouraging message: We know you are here, and we care about your needs.

In the process of delivering the simple, universal gift of food, we discover what other needs exist.

Whom do you know who has needs right now (small or large)?

_____

_____

What is one small step you could take to encourage or help that person, even though you can't solve all of his or her problems?

_____

_____

_____

Christians do not carry a fix-it tool chest so they can go about fixing all the brokenness of the world. We have instructed tongues to give others whatever message opens their ears to the gospel. Scripture uses the illustration of our planting and watering, and God's providing the harvest. We are usually unaware of what part we play in encouraging or what part we play in delivering the message of God's love.

Sometimes we cannot find words of encouragement for people during their hard times. Action alone is a great place to begin. Opportunity may come later to explain why we acted as we did.

God's usual order is for us to share with those near to us and then extend our outreach (see Acts 1:8). The disciples were to witness first in Jerusalem, then in Judea and Samaria, and then to the ends of the earth.

Using this as a guideline, answer the following:

Whom can you encourage in your close circle?

_____

_____

_____

In your neighborhood?

_____

_____

_____

In your household?

_____

_____

_____

How can you be a witness in your community or city?

_____

_____

_____

In your state? your nation? beyond?

_____

_____

_____

It's the great commission, sister. I imagine Jesus' gentle nudging: "Are you using what I have given you to reach the unreached? Or are you losing what I gave you to wake up my people? Use it or lose it." I imagine he will be quite direct with me. I seem to miss subtle nudges and need a real push. He is capable of both.

CHAPTER FOURTEEN

God Will Motivate Me to Change

The Chicago Botanical Garden is witnessing a miracle of change. Our so-called century plant is preparing to bloom. Usually a landscape ornamental, the century plant requires little water and thrives in southwest deserts and gardens. After simply vegetating for decades, a new bud appears, like an asparagus spear the size of a tree trunk. With a burst of growth it spurts up, sometimes seven inches a day, to a height of twenty to forty feet.

If the century plant is in a greenhouse, roof sections must be removed. During the growth spurt, this plant is literally on the move. Ultimately, golden blossoms appear and last for two to three weeks. The plant dies quickly then, maybe from the effort it took to grow so fast. At the same time a "pup" sprouts from the parent root system, and the process begins all over again.

The century plant is a vivid picture of God's idea of change. He creates such variety to show us that he works uniquely in all of life. Preparation, growth, blossom, rebirth. In his time.

His message: *I am the supreme specialist in timing and its results.* Change is not a lockstep product of the turning of the calendar, the circling hands of a clock, or the monotonous flicker of a digital clock's readout from one moment to the next.

I read Psalm 119:28: "Strengthen me according to your word." I want that strength instantly. If the Word makes me strong, I want to download it like I downloaded the Scriptures onto my computer. A few commands, "copy file," a soft whir—all sixty-six books in place to change my life.

Instead, he gives me only what I can act on, what I can assimilate at my stage of growth. Like the century plant, there are stages in my life when little seems to change. But God is preparing me.

And then a moment comes when the growth is visible. For some women, it's the simple act of getting through the day in spite of harsh circumstances. Victory is getting out of bed, getting dressed, putting one foot in front of the other to accomplish the necessities of survival.

For another woman it is starting an organization that proclaims or practices truth in our world. Fifteen years ago, Beverly LaHaye caught the vision of shaping government and educating women. Today she keeps 625,000 women informed on issues related to our government and our Christian faith.

Christy March began a much smaller organization in terms of numbers. She presently mentors seven teen mothers, helping them stay in school as well as parent their children. Both Beverly and Christy are growing on the right timetable, as far as God is concerned.

When will your growth result in a blossom? And what will it look like? We may never know either answer—not precisely, anyway.

Heather became pregnant at age seventeen. In despair, she attempted to take her life. While in a psychiatric hospital, she met a woman with a message of hope. The Clay Home offered her sanctuary during her pregnancy. There she learned to communicate intimately with her Creator and discovered a family for her baby. With the peace of knowing that she had made a loving and accountable choice regarding her baby's life, she placed him in good hands.

There's more. Heather graduated from high school and is now preparing for a career in social work. She wants to make a difference in the lives of other girls in psychiatric hospitals, or anywhere her Creator places her. Heather is blossoming in God's time.

Rebirth is one of God's great mysteries. When the century plant's blossoms are wilting, many feet below, ignored by the admirers of the blossoms, a pup begins from the root system. Within a tiny nub is all the potential for another century plant. Will it blossom in twenty years? thirty? forty? God alone knows. The same is true for spiritual rebirth in humans. We are transformed from having earthly living as our only goal to being connected to our Maker—women who are heaven oriented. Women who've changed.

As surely as you have committed yourself to your Creator, you will change. God guarantees it. He has placed within you all that is necessary for transformation.

If anyone is in Christ, he is a new creation; the old has gone, the new has come! (2 Corinthians 5:17)

MY RESPONSE: Pursue New Habits

Our culture teaches us that change is externally motivated—that if we want to change our habits, we need to change our surroundings or our circumstances:

- New dress → new optimism
- New weight → new self-esteem
- New job → new attitude
- New man → new potential

Scripture, by contrast, teaches that change begins *within* us. While externals may change later, whether or not they do we will be different because we are Christian women.

One habit is 100 percent internally motivated and totally within our control: spending time with God. Whether in a chair at 5:00 a.m. with open Bible, under earphones on a noisy commuter train at 7:00 p.m., or praying as we sway with a fussing baby on our shoulder at midnight, we can do it.

If we have cultivated this habit over time, but we're getting rusty, we can recalibrate and be fresh again. There is no new habit as dependable as adjusting our time and focus in worship and getting to know God. Fresh, meaningful, and relevant, our intimacy need never be on automatic pilot, just doing what we've always done.

Do you know what I mean? Stagnation versus a vitalizing relationship with God. The two result from very different habits. When we hunger for the latter, what can we do?

Try Reading a New Version of Scripture.
I remember being in awe of a new book given me by a
friend. Eight translations of the New Testament were
printed side by side. I thought the idea would never be
topped. I could not imagine more ways the Word of God
could be written. That was in 1974. I am now enjoying
The Message, which is only one of the many new para-
phrases and translations available today filling bookshelves
and challenging us to internalize Scripture in words that
speak to us.

What are two or three Scripture versions you've never
read but would like to try?

- ○ The Amplified Bible
- ○ Good News Bible, Today's English Version
- ○ The Message (Eugene Petersen)
- ○ New American Standard Bible
- ○ The New English Bible
- ○ New King James Version
- ○ New Living Translation
- ○ New Revised Standard Version
- ○ The New Testament in Modern English
  (J. B. Phillips)
- ○ Other: _____

Rewrite a Scripture Passage in Your Own Words.
Write as if no one else will see what you have written. I
include my own name and other people's names, including
my children, my friends, and my enemies. Thankfully I
look back and see that enemies of the past have not
remained so. (Thankfully I read, "If it is possible, as far as it

depends on you, live at peace with everyone," Romans 12:18.)

Get some paper and try this yourself. Here are some passages to start with: John 8:34–36; Psalm 119:48; Romans 12:1–2; Colossians 2:20; 1 Timothy 6:12.

Quiz Yourself.
Ask yourself, What does this mean to me? What difference does it make that these verses or these chapters exist?

Compare the Word and the World.
I compare Paul's characteristics of leadership in Acts with what I see demonstrated in the president of our country. I compare what Paul says in Romans with the habits I observe in myself—my struggles with guilt versus my freedom. I compare what John says in Revelation about different churches with my own life and the body of believers with whom I worship.

Focus on the Action Words.
List the action words from a passage in the Bible and write what they tell you to do. For example, for Colossians 4:2–6, this was my list:

- *Devote* myself to prayer.
- *Be watchful.*
- *Be thankful.*
- *Pray* for others.
- *Be wise* in how I act toward people who don't know Jesus.
- *Make the most* of opportunities.

- *Talk* like the woman of grace that I am.
- *Speak* with significance.

Of the action words you found, which will you focus on today? this week?

I am thankful that God does not dictate formulas for what must happen when we change. As we focus on new habits, circumstances and people may change around us. But they may not. Remember the goal: to know God. We can be sure that as we get to know God better, *we* will change. And the new woman will be better.

CHAPTER FIFTEEN

God Will Bring Glory to Himself Using Me

Great thinkers of one century are seldom as revered when their teachings have been subjected to time. Philosophers like Plato and Aristotle missed the mark of universal truth with their attitudes about slaves, children, and women.

Scientists like Einstein and Galileo made great discoveries in accurately describing complex realities in life. But their descriptions pale in significance when we ask the question, Who created the reality in the first place? Energy, gravity—whose invention are they?

One exception stands out among all the great thinkers throughout history: Jesus. He made statements that have been remembered, though as far as we know he never wrote any books or even letters.

- "Render to Caesar the things that are Caesar's and to God the things that are God's."

- "Let him among you who is without sin cast the first stone."
- "Unless you are converted, and become like little children, you shall not enter the kingdom of heaven."
- "Do unto others as you would have them do unto you."

How often I hear a witty saying and think, *I'll never forget that*. But I do.

But the words of Jesus are different. We remember them. People who do not wish to remember them still do. Why? His words go straight to our heart and stay there. Nothing he ever said has been superseded by modern science or human experience. His contemporaries brutally rejected what he said. And people still do. Any person can reject what he said, but they cannot dismiss it as belonging to a bygone era. Regarding gender, race, politics, or any aspect of life, Jesus had a distinct message that is as relevant today as when his voice carried over the hills and Sea of Galilee, the streets of Jerusalem, and the dusty roadways between the towns scattered through the wilderness called the Promised Land.

And Jesus gave credit to his Father for everything he said and did.

This same Jesus gives us these promises (see Isaiah 61:1-3):

- to bind us up when our hearts are broken
- to free us
- to comfort us when we mourn
- to give us a crown of beauty from the ashes of despair

- to give us joy instead of mourning
- to give us praise instead of despair
- to call us oaks of righteousness, a planting of the Lord for his splendor

You and I do not need to face the future with dread or an uneasy fear thinking, *How much worse can it get?* We do not need to wonder whether our daughters can live in satisfaction and comfort, given the dizzying speed of change in unknown directions. The simple truth is that Jesus loves us. He is our comfort, ours for the taking. Every word he said is relevant today, and he keeps his word. With Jesus, there is no way that our life can spin out of our comfort zone. Jesus is within us. He gives the ultimate comfort. There is no greater lover than Jesus.

MY RESPONSE: Give God All Credit

Knowing Jesus is never enough. We just *have* to do something about it. A good beginning is to review the difference he's made in our life. Then two things come naturally:

- Taking action directed toward others in response to God's action in my life
- Talking about God's action and the difference he makes

I like to use Isaiah 61:1–3, words that Jesus quoted during his earthly ministry, to guide me through memories of the difference he's made in my life.

The Spirit of the Sovereign Lord is on me, because the Lord has anointed me to preach good news to the poor. He has sent me to bind up the brokenhearted, to proclaim freedom for the captives and release from darkness for the prisoners, to proclaim the year of the Lord's favor and the day of vengeance of our God, to comfort all who mourn, and provide for those who grieve in Zion—to bestow on them a crown of beauty instead of ashes, the oil of gladness instead of mourning, and a garment of praise instead of a spirit of despair. They will be called oaks of righteousness, a planting of the Lord for the display of his splendor.

Think of a specific circumstance and recall the following:

When my heart was broken, Jesus healed me by _____

_____ .

When I grieved over _____ ,

he comforted me by _____

_____ .

From the ashes of my disaster of _____

_____ ,

he crowned me with beauty by_____

_____ .

My "oil of gladness," my source of joy, is _____

_____ .

I praise you, Jesus, because you _____

_____ .

I see your work in me evidenced by these changing characteristics:

_____

_____

_____

> I will give you the treasures of darkness, riches stored
> in secret places, so that you may know that I am the
> Lord, the God of Israel, who summons you by name.
> (Isaiah 45:3)

First we know him, then he calls us to action.

Like Elizabeth, we can say, "The Lord has done this for me" (Luke 1:25).

And if circumstances dictate that we must be silent, then our actions will still convey the message. "This is the message you heard from the beginning: We should love one another" (1 John 3:11).

Take a few minutes to write down some actions you can take, even in situations in which you're not able to speak up.

In your family:

_____

_____

_____

With your friends:

_____

_____

_____

At your job:

_____

_____

_____

In your neighborhood:

_____

_____

_____

Be encouraged to know that your life is sending a message:

- a message heard by everyone whose life you touch
- a message noted by Jesus, who will reward you and give you rest
- a message seen by the angels, who are amazed at how their Leader loves humans. And in wonder and delight, they cheer you on.

SUGGESTED READING

Miriam Adeney, *A Time for Risking* (Portland, Oreg.: Multnomah Press, 1987). This book is currently out of print, but it can be ordered from the Regent College Bookstore, 5800 University Blvd., Vancouver, B.C., Canada V6T2E4.

Kay Coles James and Jacqueline C. Fuller, *Never Forget: The Riveting Story of One Woman's Journey from the Projects to the Corridors of Power* (Grand Rapids, Mich.: Zondervan, 1993).

Ruth A. Tucker and Walter L. Liefeld, *Daughters of the Church: Women and Ministry from New Testament Times to the Present* (Grand Rapids, Mich.: Zondervan, 1987).